Jeremiah
Daring to Hope
in an Unstable World

Leader Guide

Melissa Spoelstra

Abingdon Press
Nashville

JEREMIAH: DARING TO HOPE IN AN UNSTABLE WORLD –
LEADER GUIDE

This book is printed on acid-free paper.

ISBN 978-1-4267-8894-9

14 15 16 17 18 19 20 21 22 23 — 10 9 8 7 6 5 4 3 2 1
MANUFACTURED IN THE UNITED STATES OF AMERICA

Contents

About the Author

Melissa Spoelstra is a popular women's conference speaker, Bible teacher, and writer who is madly in love with Jesus and passionate about studying God's Word and helping women of all ages to seek Christ and know Him more intimately through serious Bible study. Having a degree In Bible Theology, she enjoys teaching God's Word to the body of Christ, traveling to diverse groups and churches across the nation and recently to Nairobi, Kenya, for a women's prayer conference. Melissa has published articles in *ParentLife*, *Women's Spectrum*, and *Just Between Us* and writes a regular blog in which she shares her musings about what God is teaching her on any given day. She lives in Dublin, Ohio, with her pastor husband, Sean, and their four kids: Zach, Abby, Sara, and Rachel.

Follow Melissa:

Twitter	@MelSpoelstra
Instagram	@Daring2Hope
Facebook	@AuthorMelissaSpoelstra
Her blog	MelissaSpoelstra.com (check here also for event dates and booking information)

Introduction

The words of the prophet Jeremiah echo into our lives and culture with great relevance. This prophet found himself in a nation known for materialism, economic crisis, political globalization, and religious plurality. Sounds familiar, doesn't it? Jeremiah's message from God to the people in their uncertain times was for them to dare to hope—to put their hope in God alone instead of political alliances, material possessions, and people. The underlying message of his writings is that hope-filled living is possible even in an unstable world. It's a message that speaks to us today as well.

Rather than going through the Book of Jeremiah chapter by chapter, we will explore six hope-inspiring themes that are found throughout the chapters. As we delve into Jeremiah's writings, we'll find God calling us to lay aside our worry, fear, doubt, and bitterness and, instead, to dare to hope—not in the government, our family, a job, or even the church, but in Him alone.

Though Jeremiah's message was not a popular one and the people did not heed his warnings, my prayer is that we will not be like them. I pray that God's timeless truths from this ancient book will help us take a careful look at our lives and examine where we might be off course and how we can get back on track. I pray that we will choose to be like Jeremiah, who dared to hope even in the midst of loss and rejection and unjust treatment. Though his circumstances remained bitter, he learned to keep his heart soft and hopeful. As we study together, may we be able to say with Jeremiah, "Yet I still dare to hope / when I remember this: / The faithful love of the LORD never ends! / His mercies never cease. / Great is his faithfulness; / his mercies begin afresh each morning" (Lamentations 3:21-23).

Using This Leader Guide

This leader guide is provided to help you lead your group on this journey to find God's promise of hope for your lives and circumstances. Whether you choose to follow this guide step by step, modify its contents to meet your group's needs and preferences, or simply peruse it to find a few helpful tips, questions, and ideas, you will find in these pages some valuable tools for creating a successful group experience. Here is a quick overview of what is included:

Getting Started: This is a list of strategies, options, and introductory information that will help you ensure good organization and communication. You will want to review this material and communicate relevant information to group members prior to your group session for Week 1, either via e-mail or in an introductory session (see more about this in Getting Started). Or you might consider adding 15-30 minutes to your first session for reviewing some of these important housekeeping details. Whichever option you choose, be sure that group members have the opportunity to purchase books and complete Week 1 before your session for Week 1.

Tips for Tackling Five Common Challenges: This section includes ideas for addressing recurring issues that come up when leading a group. Every leader knows that some group dynamics can be difficult to tackle. What will you do when one person dominates the discussion or cuts off another person who is speaking? All eyes will be on you to see how you will intervene or ignore these situations. Be sure to check out these five common challenges and ideas to help when you encounter them.

Basic Leader Helps: This list of basic leader tips will help you prepare for and lead each group session.

Session Outlines: Six adaptable outlines are provided to help guide your group time each week. Each begins with a "Leader Prep" section to assist with preparation.

Digging Deeper Article Highlights: These are highlights from the full-length Digging Deeper articles found online at AbingdonWomen.com/ Jeremiah, in which you will find valuable second-level information your students do not have in their participant books, such as culture insights, background information, commentary, and so forth. (Be sure to read the full articles online prior to your group session.) As you dialogue with God about leading each session, ask Him what parts of the corresponding Digging Deeper article He might want you to share with the group. This will give participants an opportunity to continue to learn new insights in your time together each week. Feel free to point your members to the online articles in class or via e-mail, Facebook, Twitter, or other social media.

This study is designed for six weeks, with the option of adding an introductory session. (Note: If you choose to have an introductory session, Getting Started provides a helpful outline of topics you may cover. Add time for fellowship, get-acquainted activities, and prayer to round out your introductory session.) Or, if desired, you may choose to extend the study to eight or twelve weeks; see the options included in Getting Started. Again, whichever option you choose, be sure that group members have the opportunity to purchase participant books and complete Week 1 before your session for Week 1.

Each of the session outlines in this book may be used for a 60-minute, 90-minute, or 120-minute session. The following formats are offered as templates that you may modify for your group:

60-MINUTE FORMAT
Welcome/Fellowship (2 minutes)
All Play (3 minutes)
Digging Deeper Insights (4 minutes)
Prayer (1 minute)
Video (25 minutes)
Group Discussion (20 minutes)
Prayer Requests (5 minutes)

90-MINUTE FORMAT
Welcome/Fellowship (5-10 minutes)
All Play (5 minutes)
Digging Deeper Insights (4 minutes)
Prayer (1 minute)
Video (25 minutes)
Group Discussion (25 minutes)
Optional Group Activity (5-10 minutes)
Prayer Requests (10 minutes)

120-MINUTE FORMAT
Welcome/Fellowship (15-20 minutes)
All Play (5-10 minutes)
Digging Deeper Insights (4 minutes)
Prayer (1 minute)
Video (25 minutes)
Group Discussion (30 minutes)
Optional Group Activity (5-10 minutes)
Prayer Requests (15-20 minutes)

As you can see, the basic elements remain the same in each format: a welcome/fellowship time, an "All Play" icebreaker question that everyone can answer, an opportunity to share insights with the group from the week's Digging Deeper article, a video segment, group discussion, and prayer time. The 90-minute and 120-minute options offer longer times for fellowship, discussion, and prayer plus an optional group activity. If you choose not to do the group activity, you may add that time to another element of the session, such as group discussion or prayer. (See Getting Started for notes about including food, planning for childcare, and other important organizational details.)

If you are new to leading Bible studies and/or would like to have a framework to follow, the session outlines will guide you. Note that more discussion questions have been provided than you may have time to include. Before the session, choose the questions you want to cover and put a check mark beside them. Page references are provided for those questions that relate to specific questions or activities in the participant book. For these questions, invite group members to turn in their participant books to the pages indicated.

If you are a seasoned group leader looking only for a few good questions or ideas, I encourage you to take what you want and leave the rest. After all, you know your group better than I do! Ask God to show you what areas to focus on from the week's homework and use my discussion outline as a template that you can revise.

Of course, the Holy Spirit knows the content of this study (His Word) and the women in your group better than anyone, so above all I encourage you to lead this study under the Holy Spirit's direction, allowing yourself the freedom to make any changes or adaptations that are helpful or desirable.

I'm so excited that God has called you to lead a group of ladies through this study of Jeremiah. Know that I am praying for you and believing God for the work He will do through your leadership. Now, let's get started!

Melissa

Getting Started

Before your study begins, review the following introductory information that will help you ensure good organization and communication. You are encouraged to communicate relevant information (such as the dates, times, and location for group meetings; when/where/how to purchase books; details regarding childcare and food; expectations and ground rules; and an overview of the study) to group members via e-mail before your session for Week 1 or during an introductory session. If you choose to have an introductory session, use the following list as an outline of topics to cover. Add time for fellowship, get-acquainted activities, and prayer to round out your introductory session. Another option is to add 15-30 minutes to your first session for reviewing some of these housekeeping details.

1. Determine the length of your study. The basic study is designed for six weeks but also can be adapted for an eight- or twelve-week study.
   - For an eight-week study, add an introductory session and a closing celebration. In the introductory session, spend time getting to know one another, presenting basic housekeeping information, and praying together. For a closing celebration, discuss what you have learned in a special gathering that includes refreshments or perhaps a meal as well as a Jeremiah Jeopardy game (see AbindonWomen.com/Jeremiah). Or plan a group service opportunity that allows you to put into practice some of the principles of hope from the study (e.g., serve a meal in a shelter or have a workday at the home of a widow or shut-in). Whether you choose a food-centered gathering or a service activity, a closing celebration provides an excellent opportunity for ongoing groups to invite friends and reach out to others who might be interested in joining the group for a future study.
   - To allow more time for completing homework, extend the study to twelve weeks. This is especially helpful for groups with mothers of young children or women carrying a heavy work or ministry schedule. With this option, women have two weeks in which to complete each week of homework. In your group sessions, watch and discuss the video the first week; then review and discuss homework the next. Some women find this approach helps them to complete assignments and digest what they are learning.
2. Determine the length of each group session (60, 90, or 120 minutes). See the format templates outlined on page 7.

3. Decide ahead of time if you/your church will purchase participant books that group members can buy in advance of your first session or during an introductory session (if you choose to have one), or if group members will buy their own books individually. If you expect each member to buy her own book, e-mail group members purchasing information. Consider including online links as well. Be sure to allow enough time for participants to purchase books and complete the readings for Week 1 prior to your session for Week 1.

4. Create a group roster that includes each group member's name, e-mail, mailing address, and primary phone number. (Collect this information through registration, e-mail, or an introductory session.) Distribute copies of the roster to group members prior to or during your first session. A group roster enables group members to stay connected and contact one another freely as needed.

5. Make decisions about childcare and food, and communicate this information in advance. (Note: If your group is meeting for 60 minutes, you will not have time for a formal fellowship time with refreshments. You might consider having refreshments set up early and inviting women to come a few minutes before the session officially begins.) If you choose to have food, the introductory meeting is a good time to pass around a sign-up sheet. Be sure to be mindful of food allergies and provide choices that will not exclude women.

6. Let group members know what to expect. Those who have never participated in a women's Bible study group may be intimidated, scared, or unsure of what to expect. Reassure the women that they will not be put on the spot and that they may choose to share as they are comfortable. Encourage participation while fostering a "safe" environment. Laying a few basic ground rules such as these can help you achieve this kind of environment:

    • Confidentiality. Communicate that anything shared in the group is not to be repeated outside of those present in the study. Women need to feel safe to be vulnerable and authentic.

    • Sensitivity. Talk about courtesy, which includes practices such as refraining from interrupting, monopolizing, or trying to "fix" shared problems. Women want to be heard, not told what to do, when they share an issue in their lives. If they have advice to share with an individual, ask them to speak with the person privately after study. When studying God's Word, some differences of opinion are bound to arise as to interpretation and/or application. This is a good place to sharpen one another and respectfully disagree so that you may grow and understand different viewpoints. Remind the women that it's okay to question and see things differently; however, they must be kind and sensitive to the feelings of others.

    • Purpose. The primary reason you are taking time out of your busy schedules to meet together is to study the Bible. Though your group will pray for, serve, and support one another (and others, if doing a group service project), your primary focus is to study the Bible. You learn in community from one another as you draw near to God through His Word. Though you may want to plan a service or social activity during the course of your study, these times should be secondary to your study time together. If group members express a desire for the group to do more outreach, service, or socials, gently remind them of the primary reason you gather.

7. Before the study begins, provide a preview of the study's content. The preview book is an excellent way to share highlights of the study's themes. You might consider providing a copy of the preview book for each group member in advance or summarizing the highlights in an e-mail or an introductory session. Another way to whet the appetite for what is to come is to share (or read) parts of the introduction from the participant book. Be sure to mention that although Jeremiah is an Old Testament prophet who lived over 2,600 years ago, the truths in his book echo with great relevance into our day. Consider sharing a personal story that relates to the theme of the study. What has been happening in your life recently that causes you to need hope? What has been unstable in your life that is drawing you to depend more on Jesus? As you are enthusiastic and positive about getting into God's Word together, your members will catch your contagious energy.

8. If you are having an introductory session or allowing time in your first session for introductory remarks, open the floor for women to share in response to a question such as one of these:
   • What is one thing you are looking forward to in this study?
   • What is one thing you already know about Jeremiah? (For example, he was a prophet, or he wrote a book in the Old Testament. When I asked my group this question, a lot of people said, "Jeremiah was a bullfrog," which lightened the mood and got everyone laughing.)
   • What are some ways your world has felt "unstable" lately?
   • What is an area of your life in which you could really use some hope? (for example, health, relationships, finances)

9. Read the full Digging Deeper Introductory Article at AbingdonWomen.com/Jeremiah (highlights on page 23) to provide context regarding where Jeremiah fits in the biblical timeline. Share these insights in an introductory session or during the Digging Deeper Insights segment of your first session. Optional: You might consider drawing the timeline found at the end of the article on a large white board.

10. Be sure to communicate to participants that they are to read Week 1 in the participant book prior to your session for Week 1. Review the options for study found in the introduction to the participant book and encourage participants to choose the options they plan to complete and then share this information with someone in the group for accountability.

Tips for Tackling Five Common Challenges

Challenge #1: Preparation

Do you know that feeling when Bible study is in two days and you haven't even finished the lessons, much less prepared for the group session? We've all been there. When I haven't dedicated the proper time for preparation, I'm hurried, scattered, and less confident. It doesn't take hours, but it does take commitment.

I check myself with a little acronym when I prepare to lead: S-S-S. Years ago I was asked to lead a segment on teacher training for a group of VBS leaders. I remember asking the Lord, "What are the most important things to remember when we handle your Word to teach?" As I sat listening, He gave me this process of S-S-S that has stuck with me through the years. It looks like this:

S – Savior. Know your Savior. We must spend time talking, listening, and staying closely connected with Jesus in order to lead well. As we keep our walk with Him close and vibrant, we can then hear His voice about how to structure our lesson, what questions to ask, and which verses in His Word to focus on.

S – Story. Know your story. I feel the most freedom with God's truth when I have prepared thoroughly. Try not to cram in multiple days of homework at once. Let it sink into your soul by reading curiously and slowly. Go back to areas that strike you and allow God to use His Word in your heart and mind so you can teach with authenticity. Women can tell when you are flying by the seat of your pants.

S – Students. Know your students. Who are these women God has given you to shepherd? Are they struggling with finances, relationships, or body image issues? Are they mature Christ-followers who need to be challenged to go deeper in their study of God's Word or seekers who need extra explanations about where the books of the Bible are located? Most likely, you will be teaching to a wide range of backgrounds as well as emotional and spiritual maturity levels, and you will need God's wisdom and guidance to inspire them.

Challenge #2: Group Dynamics

Have you experienced that uncomfortable feeling when you ask a discussion question and a long silence settles over the group? With your eyes begging someone to break the ice, you wonder if you should let the question linger or jump in with your own answer. Other problems with group dynamics surface when

Silent Suzy never contributes to the conversation because Talking Tammy answers every question. What does a good leader do in these situations? While every group has a unique vibe, I have found these general concepts very helpful.

First of all, a good leader asks questions. One of Jesus' most effective teaching methods was asking questions. As leaders, we must be intentional askers and listeners. I try to gauge myself throughout the discussion by asking myself: "Am I doing all the talking?" When I find I am hearing my own voice too much, I make a point to ask and listen more. Even if a little silence hangs in the air, eventually someone will pipe up and share. Women learn from each other's insights and experiences; we rob them of others' comments when we monopolize as leaders.

Now what about Talking Tammy? She not only answers every question but also makes a comment after each woman shares something (often relating to one of her own experiences). Try one of these transitional statements:

- "Thanks Tammy, let's see if someone else has some insight as well."
- "Let's hear from someone who hasn't shared yet today."
- "Is there anyone who hasn't talked much today who would be willing to answer this question?"

The hope is that Talking Tammy will realize she has had a lot of floor time.

Sometimes Talking Tammy also struggles to find a stopping place in her story. Help her out by jumping in when she takes a breath, making a summary statement for her. For example, "I hear you saying that you could relate to Jeremiah's struggle with his friend since you had a similar experience. Anyone else find that passage resonating with you?" Occasionally I have had to take someone aside in a loving way and address her amount of talking. Pray hard and be gentle, but address the issue. As a leader, you must keep in mind the good of the group as a whole.

Sometimes even more challenging than Talking Tammy is Silent Suzy. How do we get Silent Suzy to talk without singling her out? Here are some ideas:

- If she is new to the study, let her feel safe and get comfortable. Never call on her to pray out loud or single her out with a pointed question. I once said, "I want to know what Suzy thinks about this." All eyes turned on her, and I'll never forget the tears welling in the corners of her eyes as she said she wasn't comfortable being called on. She didn't come back to the group after that incident. How I wish I could have taken those words back. I learned a valuable lesson from that Silent Suzy—don't push!
- Listen with recall as she answers the All Play question that everyone is asked to answer. Watch for an opportunity to talk about something she has shared with a follow-up question that doesn't pry.
- Take her out for coffee and get to know her. With time, she might warm up and begin to contribute to the discussion. Through a deepened relationship, you'll get a better read on whether you should encourage her to talk.

Challenge #3: Prayer Requests

How often do we run out of time when sharing prayer requests, leaving us no time to actually pray? How do you handle those women who aren't comfortable praying out loud? What if your group has fifteen to thirty women, and just listening to everyone's prayer request takes half an hour?

It's so important to take the time to hear what is going on in each other's lives and to pray for one another. Here are some creative ideas I have learned from others to help keep prayer time fresh:

- As women enter the room, direct them to take an index card and write their prayer request on it. Then during prayer time, each woman can read her request aloud, already having thought through it, and pass it to the woman on the right for her to keep in her Bible as a reminder to pray for the request until they meet again.
- Have someone record the prayer requests and e-mail them to the group.
- If you have a small group, set a timer for one or two minutes. Lightheartedly tell each woman that she has one or two minutes to share her request so that each woman can have a turn. (You might want to flip it over again if tears accompany the request.)
- If you have more than ten women, divide into two or three groups for prayer. Assign a leader who will facilitate, keep the group on track, and follow up. Sometimes our prayer group has gone out for breakfast together or gathered in someone's home to watch the teaching video again.
- Have women pick one or two partners and split into small groups of two or three to share prayer requests and pray for each other.
- Have an open time of popcorn prayer. This means let women spontaneously pray one-sentence prayers as they feel led.
- After everyone shares requests, ask each woman to pray for the woman on her right. Clearly say that if anyone is uncomfortable praying out loud, she can pray silently and then squeeze the hand of the woman next to her.
- Another option is to close the group in prayer yourself or ask a few women who are comfortable praying in front of others to pray for the requests mentioned. Provide encouragement by reminding the group that prayer is talking with God, and that there is no right or wrong way to have a conversation with our Creator. But always be sensitive to others and affirm that they will not be looked down on if they don't like to pray out loud.

Making a change in your prayer time occasionally keeps it from becoming routine or boring. Talking with Jesus should be fresh and real. Taking an intentional, thoughtful approach to this important time of your study will add great value to your time together.

Challenge #4: Developing Leaders

Women's Bible study groups are a great avenue for fulfilling the 2-2-2 principle, which comes from 2 Timothy 2:2: "You have heard me teach things that have been confirmed by many reliable witnesses. Now teach these truths to other trustworthy people who will be able to pass them on to others." As a leader, God calls us to help raise up other leaders.

Is there a woman in your group who is capable of leading? How can you come alongside her and help equip her to be an even better leader? Wonderful women have invested in me through the 2-2-2 principle, even before I knew that term. As an apprentice, I watched them lead. They gave me opportunities to try leading without handing the full reins over to me. Then they coached and corrected me. I have since had the privilege of mentoring several apprentices in my Bible study group and watching them go on to lead their own groups.

Here is the 2-2-2 principle as laid out by Dave and Jon Ferguson in their book *Exponential*.[1] (My notes are added within brackets.)

- I DO. You WATCH. We TALK.
- I DO. You HELP. We TALK. [Have your apprentice lead a prayer group or an activity or portion of the session.]
- You DO. I HELP. We TALK. [Ask your apprentice to lead one session with you assisting with facilitation alongside her.]
- You DO. I WATCH. We TALK. [Give your apprentice full ownership for leading a session and resist the urge to jump in and take over.]
- You DO. Someone else WATCHES. [As God leads over time, encourage your apprentice to start her own Bible study group.]

My mentor and I led a Bible study group together for years. As the group grew larger, we both sensed God leading us to multiply the group, forming two groups. It was painful as we missed studying and working with each other. However, God blessed and used both groups to reach more women. Then a woman in my group felt called to lead her own study. She worried that no one would come to her group. She asked many questions as we worked through the 2-2-2 principle. Her first group meeting included eighteen women who now, four years later, still love meeting together. I just saw a picture of them on Facebook having a Christmas brunch, and I praised God for all that He is doing.

From our one study there are now over five groups of women that meet regularly to study God's Word. This kind of growth begins with commitment to share leadership, follow the 2-2-2 principle, and multiply so that more women can grow in their walk with Christ. Don't miss the opportunity to develop new leaders with intentionality as you model and encourage other women to use their gifts.

Challenge #5: Reaching Out

How do you welcome new women into the group? This is especially tough if yours is an ongoing group that has had the same women in it for years. Also, what about those who are finding their way back to God? Are they welcome in the group? While the purpose of the group is primarily Bible study, I've seen the Great Commission of making disciples happen many times through women's groups that meet for Bible study. God's Word will do the transforming work in their lives through the Holy Spirit. We are called to reach out by investing and inviting. Here are some ways a leader can help create an open group:

- End each Bible study with a closing celebration brunch, encouraging the women to bring food and friends:
  1. Have an open time when women can share how God worked in their lives through the Bible study.
  2. Have a woman share her testimony of how she came to understand the gospel and how it has been transforming her life recently.
  3. Bring in a speaker from outside the group to share a testimony.
  4. Have fun! We play a group game (for instance, Fishbowl, Pictionary, or Loaded Questions) and have a white elephant jewelry exchange at Christmas. Women who might think Bible study is a foreign concept can see that you are just regular women in pursuit of a supernatural God.
- Leave a chair empty in the group and pray for God to show you someone who needs a group of women she can study the Bible alongside.
- Though the main purpose of the group is Bible study, consider doing a service project together that you can invite other women to participate in (schedules permitting). Our group has made personal care bags for the homeless and also adopted a family at Christmas, which included going shopping for the gifts and wrapping them together. Depending on where God is leading your group, serving together can help put hands and feet to the truths you are learning.
- Socials outside of Bible study also provide an opportunity to invite friends as a nonthreatening transition. While the focus of your group is much more than social, planning an occasional social event can be a good way to forge deeper connections. Our Bible study group has gone bowling together, had a backyard barbecue, and planned a girls' night out at a local restaurant. These times together not only help women to get to know one another better but also give them a great chance to invite friends. These same friends who attend a social might later try a Bible study session once they have made connections with some of the women in the group.

---

1. Dave and Jon Ferguson, *Exponential: How You and Your Friends Can Start a Missional Church Movement* (Grand Rapids, MI: Zondervan, 2010), 58, 63.

Basic Leader Helps

Preparing for the Sessions

- Check out your meeting space before each group session. Make sure the room is ready. Do you have the equipment and supplies you need? (See the list of materials needed in each session outline.)
- Pray for your group and each group member by name. Ask God to work in the life of every woman in your group.
- Read and complete the week's readings in the participant book, review the session outline in the leader guide, and read the Digging Deeper article for the week. Put a check mark beside the discussion questions you want to cover and make any notes you want to share during discussion.

Leading the Sessions

- Personally greet each woman as she arrives. If desired, take attendance using your group roster.
- As you begin, ask the women to turn off or silence their cell phones.
- Begin and end on time.
- Encourage everyone to participate, but don't put anyone on the spot. Be prepared to offer a personal example or answer if no one else responds.
- Facilitate but don't dominate. Remember that if you talk most of the time, group members may tend to listen rather than to engage.
- Try not to interrupt, judge, or minimize anyone's comments or input.
- Remember that you are not expected to be the expert or have all the answers. Acknowledge that all of you are on this journey together, with the Holy Spirit as your leader and guide.
- Encourage discussion but don't be timid about calling time on a particular question and moving ahead in order to stay on schedule.
- Be prepared for some women to want to hang out and talk at the end. If you need everyone to leave by a certain time, communicate this at the beginning of the session. If you are meeting in a church during regularly scheduled activities or have arranged for childcare, be sensitive to the agreed upon ending time.
- Thank the women for coming, and let them know you're looking forward to seeing them next time.

Week 1

RAISING THE WHITE FLAG

Surrender

Leader Prep

Memory Verse

When I discovered your words, I devoured them.
They are my joy and my heart's delight,
for I bear your name,
O Lord God of Heaven's Armies.

Jeremiah 15:16

Digging Deeper

If you did not have an introductory session, read the Digging Deeper Introductory Article, "Where Does Jeremiah Fit in the Biblical Timeline?" Also read Digging Deeper Week 1, "The Profile of a Prophet." Note any interesting facts or insights that you would like to share with the group. (See pages 23-25 for highlights; read the full articles online at AbingdonWomen.com/Jeremiah.)

Materials Needed

- *Jeremiah* DVD and DVD player
- Stick-on nametags and markers (optional)
- Empty basket, index cards, pens or pencils (Group Activity)
- Recording of "My Hope Is in You" by Aaron Shust, device and speaker for playing (optional – Group Activity)
- Index cards (optional – Prayer Requests)

Session Outline

Note: Refer to the format templates on page 7 for suggested time allotments.

Welcome

Offer a word of welcome to the group. If time allows and you choose to provide food, invite the women to enjoy refreshments and fellowship. (Groups meeting for 60 minutes may want to have a time for food and fellowship before the official start time.) Be sure to watch the clock and move to the All Play icebreaker at the appropriate time.

All Play

Ask each group member to respond briefly to this question: *During your school years (K-12), what did you want to be when you grew up?*

Read aloud or paraphrase:

Jeremiah grew up being groomed to be a priest like his father before him. I'm sure being a prophet proclaiming controversial messages that would alienate his family was not on his list of career choices. Did things turn out like you thought they would as you dreamed of what you wanted to be when you grew up? (Pause briefly for responses.) Let's see what it actually meant to be a prophet of God in Jeremiah's day.

Digging Deeper Insights

Share with the group the insights you gained from the Digging Deeper article(s). If you did not have an introductory session, you might consider drawing the chronological timeline found at the end of the Introductory Article on a large white board before the session begins (optional). Also highlight interesting facts you learned about biblical prophets. If you choose, encourage group members to read the full article(s) online (AbingdonWomen.com/Jeremiah).

Prayer

Before playing the video segment, ask God to prepare the group to receive His Word and to hear His voice.

Video

Play the video for Week 1. Invite participants to complete the Video Viewer Guide for Week 1 in the participant book as they watch.

Group Discussion

Video Discussion Questions

- What are some things we are often tempted to make our "safe place"?
- What happens to us when we rely on human strength rather than on God? How are we like a stunted shrub in the desert? How have you experienced this in your own life?
- What happens to us when we surrender to God, draw near to Him, and make Him our hope and our confidence? How are we like a tree planted by the riverbank? How have you experienced this in your own life?
- How can we "plant" ourselves next to God? What role does surrender play in this?
- According to Jeremiah's words in Lamentations 3:21-23, why can we dare to hope?

Participant Book Discussion Questions

Note: Page references are provided for those questions that relate to specific questions or activities in the participant book.

Before you begin, invite volunteers to look up the following Scriptures and be prepared to read them aloud when called upon. You might want to write each of the Scripture references on a separate note card or sticky note that you can hand out.

Scriptures: 2 Peter 1:19-21; Matthew 5:17-19; Luke 9:23; Jeremiah 20:7-18; Matthew 5:1-12; Jeremiah 15:10-18; Jeremiah 17:5-8

Day 1: No Excuses

- Have volunteers read aloud 2 Peter 1:19-21 and Matthew 5:17-19. Review your comments related to these verses and the quote from Frances Schaeffer (page 11). How do these words inspire you to study the Book of Jeremiah? What relevance do you think Jeremiah's book has for us as believers today?
- As you saw God's calling and encouragement to Jeremiah in Chapter 1 of his book, how did that encourage you about God's calling and plan for you? Have you recently heard God calling you to do something?
- What are some excuses you have made when God has called you? (page 13)
- Is anyone willing to share some of her big dreams and aspirations and/ or the next steps of obedience God may have revealed to you in prayer? (page 15)

Day 2: Surrender and Popularity

- What was your popularity level in high school? Do you think cliques and popularity still play a role in the age group you find yourself now? Why or why not?
- Have someone read aloud Luke 9:23. How does God's message of surrender in Jeremiah's prophecy parallel the gospel of Christ?
- When you have followed God, have your trials ever seemed to increase? (page 19)

Day 3: Confirmation

- In what ways has God confirmed His leading in your life? (people, Scripture, circumstances, and so on)
- Has God ever given you instructions and you could get no peace until you followed through? What did God ask you to do? Why did you resist? What did you experience when you obeyed? (page 22)
- Have someone read aloud Jeremiah 20:7-18. Review Jeremiah's hope and despair statements. (page 21) How can you relate to these statements in your life right now?
- Give some examples of how God's message of hope through surrender contrasts our modern world's view of winning at all costs.

Day 4: Defining Success

- Look at your true/false responses on page 26. Can you relate with Jeremiah because of a current struggle with frustration or depression in your life? Share as you are willing.

- How did you fill in the blank: "If I could just _____, then I would be happy with my life"? (page 28)
- Have someone read aloud Matthew 5:1-12. How does God describe the "blessed" life or individual, and how does this differ from our culture's definition of success? (page 29)
- How does the world's definition of success creep into your thinking?

Day 5: White Flag Anxiety

- Have someone read aloud Jeremiah 15:10-18. What are your current complaints before your God? How did God's promises to Jeremiah bring you comfort and faith regarding your own current complaints? (page 31)
- What action step did you check that you could take to devour God's Word more fully? (page 32) (Perhaps encourage each group member to share her step with one other woman in the group for accountability.)
- Have someone read aloud Jeremiah 17:5-8. According to the illustration in these verses, where is your tree planted right now? Is it close to the riverbank, in the desert, or somewhere in between? What needs to change in your life to move your tree closer to the riverbank? (page 37)

Optional Group Activity (for a session longer than 60 minutes)

Place an empty basket at the front of the room and provide index cards and pens or pencils for each participant. Ask each woman to think of one thing that is keeping her tree from being planted right next to the riverbank and to write it on a card. Say: *What is hindering a closer walk with Jesus in your life? Is there a person, an addiction, an activity, or some type of idol that is elevated above God? God wants to have first place in your life. Write it on an index card, offer it up to God, and then rip it up and put it in the basket at the front of the room. This will be a physical illustration of a spiritual desire to let nothing stand in the way of a close walk with your God.*

During this time of reflection, you might want to play a song in the background. "My Hope Is in You" by Aaron Shust is a wonderful praise song that uses Jeremiah's illustration of the tree as its theme. You might download it and play it through a Bluetooth speaker if you have one. (This would be a good thing to ask your apprentice leader to help with!)

Prayer Requests

End by inviting the group members to share prayer requests and pray for one another. Use index cards, popcorn prayer, or another prayer technique included in Tips for Tackling Five Common Challenges (page 14) to lead this time with intentionality and sensitivity.

DIGGING DEEPER
INTRODUCTORY ARTICLE
HIGHLIGHTS

Where Does Jeremiah Fit in the Biblical Timeline?

See AbingdonWomen.com/Jeremiah for the full article and a chronology timeline.

To best understand the message of Jeremiah, let's use broad strokes to review some basic Bible history. The first five books of the Bible (Genesis through Deuteronomy) are referred to as the Pentateuch and tell the story of the Creation, the Fall, the Flood, the giving of the Law, and the captivity of the Jews in Egypt. These are the stories of the patriarchs Abraham, Isaac, and Jacob (Israel) and others such as Noah, Joseph, and Moses. The Pentateuch ends with Moses' death and the people at the end of their forty years of wilderness wandering.

After Moses died, Joshua led the Israelites to conquer and inhabit the Promised Land of Canaan. There the people fell into a cycle of disobedience that inevitably led to punishment followed by repentance; but, soon after, they would repeat the pattern of sin, punishment, and obedience. This was the time of the judges. The books of Joshua, Judges, and Ruth tell of these times.

The next time period is that of the kings and prophets. Samuel anointed the first king of Israel (Saul). The books of First and Second Samuel record the stories of Saul, David, and Solomon as kings of the united nation of Israel. In First and Second Kings and First and Second Chronicles we read the stories of the Divided Kingdom.

During the Divided Kingdom, Israel had nineteen evil kings. God sent many prophets to warn the Israelites of their sin, but they were conquered by the Assyrians in 722 B.C. because of their disobedience. God sent prophets to proclaim His Word to try to draw them back to Him (for example, Isaiah, Ezekiel, Daniel, and Jeremiah).

Jeremiah, known as the "weeping prophet," came on the scene during the reign of King Josiah in the Southern Kingdom of Judah to warn the people of their idolatry, apathy, and disobedience. He delivered God's messages telling them to surrender to the king of Babylon. Jeremiah foretold the return of God's people to Jerusalem from their exile in Babylon. His ministry lasted some forty-plus years.

DIGGING DEEPER WEEK 1 HIGHLIGHTS

The Profile of a Prophet

*See AbingdonWomen.com/Jeremiah for the full article
and a prophet comparison chart.*

God called men and women as prophets with the specific purpose of delivering God's messages to His people. Often the prophets are divided into categories based on when their ministry occurred.

1. The Standard Preexilic Prophets. "The prophets included in this group are Isaiah, Jeremiah, Ezekiel, Hosea, Joel, Amos, Micah, Habakkuk, and Zephaniah. They are described as 'preexilic' because their times are located prior to (or during) the destruction of Jerusalem and the exile of 586 B.C."[1] These prophets are referred to as standard because their messages contain similar themes of disobedience, judgment, and hope.[2]

2. The Non-standard Preexilic Prophets. Obadiah, Nahum, and Jonah are preexilic prophets, but they address foreign nations instead of Israel and Judah.[3]

3. The Postexilic Prophets and Daniel. "Typically, Haggai, Zechariah, and Malachi are identified as the 'postexilic' prophets because they delivered their messages after the return of the exiles to Jerusalem following the Babylonian/Persian exile."[3] Daniel gets placed in this group because his message lines up most closely with the postexilic prophets.

Not all prophets authored Old Testament books. The early prophetic accounts appear in First and Second Samuel, Kings, and Chronicles. The prophets who wrote Old Testament books fall into two categories of Major and Minor Prophets. *Major* or *minor* reveals nothing of their importance but speaks to the length of their writings. Isaiah, Jeremiah, Ezekiel, and Daniel retain major prophet status simply because their books are longer.

Prophets lived in direct communication with the Creator God who knows all things past, present, and future. These forthtellers spoke the future as the Lord directed them. Prophets often recorded visions of common objects that had spiritual meanings. They used demonstrative physical actions to communicate the messages God gave them.

"The word *prophet* is from the Hebrew . . . (*nabi*). The derivation of this word is a matter of controversy, but the essential idea in the word is that of an *authorized spokesman*."[4] One source explains, "A person became a prophet by becoming aware that God was speaking to him and having to transmit the message. The consciousness came in different ways and was communicated through the prophet's own unique personality. Jeremiah says simply that the hand of the Lord touched him and words were put into his mouth (Jeremiah 1:9)."[5]

The prophet's words usually included three elements:

Past Sin – The prophet specifically named the sins of the nation.

Present Responsibility – The prophet issued a call to repentance and described the consequences of continuing in sin.

Future Hope – The prophet gave the hope of blessing for those who turned from sin and back to the Lord.

The messages of the prophets related to the people of their own times and circumstances and also echoed far into the future, with many messianic prophecies quoted in the New Testament.

Jesus stands out from among the rest as prophet, priest, and king. Much more than just a prophet delivering God's message, Jesus fulfills what all the other prophets spoke. Revelation 19:10b says, "For the essence of *prophecy* is to give a clear witness for *Jesus*" (emphasis added). He is the only way to true relationship with God. As we follow and trust Him, Jesus helps us grow and calls us to speak His message to others.

---

1. J. Daniel Hays, *The Message of the Prophets* (Grand Rapids: Zondervan, 2010), 63.

2. Ibid. 69.

3. Ibid. 71.

4. From "The Major Prophets," https://bible.org/seriospage/major-prophets.

5. Ralph Gower, *The New Manners and Customs of Bible Times* (Chicago: Moody, 2005), 330.

Week 2

RECOGNIZING COUNTERFEITS AND THE REAL DEAL

Idolatry

Memory Verse

> *Idols are worthless; they are ridiculous lies!*
> *On the day of reckoning they will all be destroyed.*
> *But the God of Israel is no idol!*
> *He is the Creator of everything that exists,*
> *including Israel, his own special possession.*
> *The LORD of Heaven's Armies is his name!*
>
> Jeremiah 10:15-16

Digging Deeper

Read Digging Deeper Week 2, "The Queen of Heaven," and note any interesting facts or insights you would like to share with the group. (See pages 32-33 for highlights; read the full article online at AbingdonWomen.com/Jeremiah.)

Materials Needed

- *Jeremiah* DVD and DVD player
- Stick-on nametags and markers (optional)
- Small poster board (1 for each small group/pair) and markers (Group Activity)
- Index cards (optional – Prayer Requests)

Session Outline

Note: Refer to the format template on page 7 for suggested time allotments.

Welcome

Offer a word of welcome to the group. If time allows and you choose to provide food, invite the women to enjoy refreshments and fellowship. (Groups meeting for 60 minutes may want to have a time for food and fellowship before the official start time.) Be sure to watch the clock and move to the All Play icebreaker at the appropriate time.

All Play

Ask each group member to respond briefly to these questions: *What piece of jewelry do you especially enjoy wearing lately? What does it look like and what do you like about it?* (If some ladies say they don't wear any jewelry at all, ask them to describe the piece of clothing in their closet that they like the most and tell why.)

Read aloud or paraphrase:

This week we saw God use jewelry as an illustration of things we value. We also talked about the story of the fake pearls in which the little girl was asked by a loving father to give up something she treasured. He may have seemed unkind at first, asking her to give up something that brought her such pleasure. However, we saw that he wanted to offer her something better—something real and lasting—and this helps us understand God's heart in asking us to give up things that seem good in the moment but ultimately don't fill the ache inside. Have any of you ever loved some particular piece of jewelry that eventually got lost, was broken, or turned funny colors over time? (Pause briefly for responses.) God wants to offer us real and lasting peace in a relationship with Him that never fades or falls apart. Let's see how the women of Judah turned to a god called the Queen of Heaven and how we can relate with their quest for beauty and power.

Digging Deeper Insights

Share insights from Digging Deeper Week 2, "The Queen of Heaven." You might consider mentioning the three possible goddesses worshiped in Canaan, Egypt, and Assyria/Babylon that might be the inspiration behind this Queen of Heaven that the women of Judah worshiped. Perhaps highlight the similar thirst for beauty and power among all three goddesses and ask: *How do women in our culture also look for identity in beauty and power?* If you choose, encourage group members to read the full article online (AbingdonWomen.com/Jeremiah).

Prayer

Before playing the video segment, ask God to prepare the group to receive His Word and to hear His voice.

Video

Play the video for Week 2. Invite participants to complete the Video Viewer Guide for Week 2 in the participant book as they watch.

Group Discussion

Video Discussion Questions

- In Jeremiah 2:10-13, what did God say His people had done? In what ways are we like the people of Judah?
- What are some of the counterfeits that we often look to for satisfaction? How are the modern idols in our lives like cracked cisterns?
- Why does God want us to look to Him alone for satisfaction? Why is God's living water the only thing that can truly satisfy?
- Why do we need to drink deeply and frequently in order to quench our spiritual thirst? Why do you think we tend to resist this? What can help us push past our "not wanting"?
- Which pitcher are you more like today—filled with sugary substitutes, empty, or overflowing with living water?

Participant Book Discussion Questions

> *Note: Page references are provided for those questions that relate to specific questions or activities in the participant book.*

Before you begin, invite volunteers to look up the following Scriptures and be prepared to read them aloud when called upon. You might want to write each of the Scripture references on a separate note card or sticky note that you can hand out.

Scriptures: Exodus 20:4-6; Exodus 23:33; Jeremiah 2:32; Jeremiah 2:4-8; 1 John 5:20-21; John 4:13-14; Jeremiah 51:17-19; Romans 8:1; Jeremiah 7:3; Jeremiah 22:16; James 1:27; 1 Timothy 6:6-10; Jeremiah 32:17

Day 1: Forgetfulness

- Have volunteers read aloud Exodus 20:4-6 and Exodus 23:33. Out of the list of commandments, God gives the most details about idolatry. We learned that the word for idolatry can mean a trap. In what ways can idolatry become a trap in the lives of women today?
- Have someone read aloud Jeremiah 2:32. God gives two examples to contrast the forgetfulness of His people. Describe the two women and the items they never forget. (page 43)
- After reading about the people of Judah turning to things they could taste, touch, feel, and control, how did you answer this question: What are some practices, relationships, or objects in our culture that can become idolatrous when they draw our hearts away from God? (page 45)
- How could you utilize the same tools you use to remember other things to help you keep God at the center of your life? (page 45)

Day 2: Spotting a Fake

- How did the story of the girl with the fake pearls impact you? Can you relate this story to anything you feel God is asking you to give to Him right now?
- Have someone read aloud Jeremiah 2:4-8. What question did the people of Judah fail to ask? (page 47) What is one way you could be more proactive in asking this question in your current circumstances?
- On page 48 we find two forms of idolatry. What are they? Which do you think is more difficult to identify and why?
- Have someone read aloud 1 John 5:20-21. Is anyone willing to tell about your experience of writing down your own idol and burning the piece of paper? (page 49) You don't have to share what you wrote; just tell how the experience impacted you.
- According to the quote by Timothy Keller, what can help us recognize when too much of a good thing has become an idol in our own lives? (page 50) Do you agree or disagree with him?
- Have volunteers read aloud John 4:13-14 and Jeremiah 51:17-19. Then read the paragraph on page 53 that begins "In order to stop our apathetic satisfaction with substitutes, we need to find satisfaction in the true Creator God. . . . " Remind group members that we often learn from

each other's experiences. Ask them to keep that in mind as they answer this question: What are some things that have helped you focus on God and resist the temporary gratification of counterfeits?

Day 3: Counterfeit Consequences

- How did you summarize your findings on the chart on page 54? (What things did God want His people to stop, and what would be the consequences for their actions if they did not stop?) How do our idolatrous distractions compare and contrast to those of Jeremiah's day? (page 55)
- In the activity on pages 56-57, what connections did you find between our idolatry and God's anger? How did you summarize God's reactions when we worship anything except Him?
- How did you answer these questions: Has today's lesson changed your attitude about how seriously God takes our sin? If so, how? (page 58)
- Have volunteers read aloud Romans 8:1 and Jeremiah 7:3. How do God's mercy and love fit with God's serious attitude toward sin? (This is a great opportunity to talk about the gospel message.)

Day 4: Resources

- According to page 60, what five people groups did God name in the three passages in Jeremiah? As we look at our own culture, what categories would you add to describe those who are often "forgotten"?
- Have someone read aloud Jeremiah 22:16 and James 1:27. How does our treatment of others reflect our relationship with God?
- After reading the story of Vicky Talbot, how did you say you would feel if she were your daughter or sister? (pages 61–62) How did this story give you clarity about God's emotions when others offer "superficial treatments" for His people's "mortal wound" (spiritually speaking)?
- How do you see greed fleshed out in the circles you run in? (page 63)
- Have someone read aloud 1 Timothy 6:6-10. How have you witnessed the love of money causing sorrow? Did God reveal anything specific about your spending habits—the material things that have the most lure in your heart and a non-necessity item that would be difficult to cut from your budget? (page 64) Share as you are willing with the group.

Day 5: Making a Fake

- Have group members turn in their Bibles to Jeremiah 10:1-16. Have each woman read one verse, going around the room until all the verses have been read. (You may have to go around again if your group is small.) How would you sum up in one sentence the key difference between idols and God? (page 66)

- Have someone read aloud Jeremiah 32:17. How does the last line of this verse, which is about nothing being too difficult for God, strike you? Is there anything going on in your life right now that requires faith and prayer for you to believe that it is not too difficult for God to work out?

Optional Group Activity (for a session longer than 60 minutes)

In order to cling to God instead of counterfeits, we need to know and understand more about our God. Have the women divide into groups of 3-4. (If your group is small, do this activity in pairs.) Give each group or pair a small piece of posterboard and a few markers. In the middle they are to draw a circle and write "God" inside it. Then instruct the groups or pairs to draw lines that extend out from the circle and connect to smaller circles in which they write traits or character qualities of God. They can identify as many or as few traits as they would like. Encourage them to use their Bibles for ideas. Allow about five minutes. After time is up, tell them they have another five minutes to discuss the following:

1. Pick one of the traits you identified; think of a verse or Bible story that illustrates that truth about God that you can share with everyone.
2. Ask someone in the group to tell about a time that God personally showed or demonstrated one of the traits listed on the poster in her life. It can be the same trait from #1 or a different one. The example can be anything big or small— a time she felt God's love, provision, or protection, and so forth.

Bring the full group back together. Have each group or pair show their poster and share their responses with the group.

Ask each group or pair to decide who should take the poster home—perhaps the woman who shared about a personal experience. Challenge each woman to pick one trait on the poster to praise God for this week. Offer a prayer, praising God for His many attributes and acknowledging that idols do not compare to Him!

Prayer Requests

End by inviting group members to share prayer requests and pray for one another. Use index cards, popcorn prayer, or another prayer technique included in "Tips for Tackling Five Common Challenges" (page 14) to lead this time with intentionality and sensitivity.

DIGGING DEEPER
WEEK 2 HIGHLIGHTS

The Queen of Heaven

See AbingdonWomen.com/Jeremiah for the full article.

> *"No wonder I am so angry! Watch how the children gather wood and the fathers build sacrificial fires. See how the women knead dough and make cakes to offer to the Queen of Heaven. And they pour out liquid offerings to their other idol gods!"*
>
> Jeremiah 7:18

> *Then all the women present and all the men who knew that their wives had burned incense to idols—a great crowd of all the Judeans living in northern Egypt and southern Egypt—answered Jeremiah, "We will not listen to your messages from the LORD! We will do whatever we want. We will burn incense and pour out liquid offerings to the Queen of Heaven just as much as we like."*
>
> Jeremiah 44:15-17a, b

From the very beginning of Jeremiah's ministry in Chapter 7 to the very end of his book, with a remnant of Judeans living in Egypt after Jerusalem has been destroyed, we see women leading the charge in the worship of the Queen of Heaven. Who is she? Did they make her up?

Judah and Israel were set apart as the only nations that worshiped just one God. All of the surrounding nations of Egypt, Assyria, Babylon, and the Canaanite countries had numerous gods, and none of them were exclusive. "Polytheistic religions are flexible and readily accept foreign gods into their pantheons, either as new gods or through identification with existing gods."[1]

So when looking at the Queen of Heaven, the women of Judah could have taken her from the Canaanite Astarte (the evening star goddess of sex and war), the goddess daughter Astarte of the Egyptian sun god, Ra, who was a warrior god, or the Assyrian/Babylonian goddess Ishtar who ruled over love, sexuality, and war.[2]

All of these cultures influenced the people of Judah. God often warned them not to be influenced by the pagan gods of the Canaanites. Egypt held Judah as a vassal nation during Jeremiah's ministry. The Babylonians came in, taking people and treasures and eventually destroying Jerusalem. Women might have seen the Babylonians' power and thought their gods to be of great power because of their military success. No matter the exact name or identity of this goddess, we find each option very similar in her appeal.

Idols of love and power also tempt us today as we fight our culture to give God first place in our lives. God loves beauty because He created a beautiful world. He also likes new things; Revelation 21:5 says that He is going to make all things new. However, we must guard against the Queen of Heaven's lure to worship beauty, love, and sex. Everywhere we turn we hear messages declaring that we must go to great lengths to look good. The women of Judah lived during a time of financial crisis much as we do, but they baked special cakes, burned incense, and poured out wine in hopes of finding love and control.

We also use our resources to buy pricey cosmetics, expensive gym memberships, new clothes, Botox, and even plastic surgery in order to draw the attention of others. Looking good is not wrong, but we all know when we've crossed the line into an obsession. The women of Judah "exchanged their glorious God for worthless idols!" (Jeremiah 2:11). We would be wise to learn from them so that we are not tempted to do the same.

The Queen of Heaven was a goddess of love and also a goddess of war. The Judean women bought into the lie that she possessed the power to give them victory. We face many battles ourselves. Our desire for control leads to many fears and anxieties and becomes idolatry when things must always go our way with our husbands, children, jobs, friendships, and even ministries. Power drugs us to desire more. Though we are not baking cakes or pouring out drinks as the women of Judah did, we worship Astarte or Ishtar every time we set beauty, sex, and power above God in our hearts.

---

1. L. de Blois and R.J. van der Spek, *An Introduction to the Ancient World* (New York: Routledge, 2008), 48.

2. Jack R. Lundbom, *The Anchor Bible*, Jeremiah 1-20 (New York: Doubleday, 1999), 476.

Week 3
OPENING OUR EARS
Listening

Memory Verse

"Ask me and I will tell you remarkable secrets you do not know about things to come."

Jeremiah 33:3

Digging Deeper

Read Digging Deeper Week 3, "Cultural Cues," and note any interesting facts or insights you would like to share with the group. (See pages 40-42 for highlights; read the full article online at AbingdonWomen.com/Jeremiah.)

Materials Needed

- *Jeremiah* DVD and DVD player
- Stick-on nametags and markers (optional)
- Individual Play-Doh® containers for each group member (optional – Group Activity)
- Recording of "The Potter's Hand" by Darlene Zschech, or another song (optional – Group Activity)
- Index cards (optional – Prayer Requests)

Session Outline

Note: Refer to the format templates on page 7 for suggested time allotments.

Welcome

Offer a word of welcome to the group. If time allows and you choose to provide food, invite the women to enjoy refreshments and fellowship. (Groups meeting for 60 minutes may want to have a time for food and fellowship before the official start time.) Be sure to watch the clock and move to the All Play icebreaker at the appropriate time.

All Play

Ask each group member to respond briefly to this question: *Curious George was a favorite childhood book of the author. What was one of your favorite childhood books or series? What special memories do you have of reading the book or listening to someone reading it to you?*

Read aloud or paraphrase:

This week we learned about listening. Many of us have read stories to young children and struggled when they fidgeted or whispered to each other. Have you ever been on the phone with someone but you could tell their attention was really focused elsewhere? (Pause briefly for responses.) God wants us to listen with attention so that we can hear what He is trying to tell us. In order to understand the culture of the Judeans of Jeremiah's day and to draw some parallels with our own society, let's take a closer look at four areas of life. The people of Judah struggled to listen to God partly because they were distracted with other things politically, economically, socially, and even religiously. Let me share with you the highlights of what I learned from the Digging Deeper article for this week, "Cultural Cues."

Digging Deeper Insights

Share insights from Digging Deeper Week 3, "Cultural Cues." You might consider sharing a brief point from each section regarding the nation of Judah:

- Economic Crisis (national debt to other nations through paying tribute to Egypt, Assyria, Babylon)
- Political Globalization (a move away from nationalism and toward a blending of all cultures)

- Social Materialism (a greed for more that rules the lives of people)
- Religious Pluralism (everything is celebrated except religion that claims ultimate truth)

Ask: *How do you see similarities in our culture?* If you choose, encourage group members to read the full article online (AbingdonWomen.com/Jeremiah).

Prayer

Before playing the video segment, ask God to prepare the group to receive His Word and to hear His voice.

Video

Play the video for Week 3. Invite participants to complete the Video Viewer Guide for Week 3 in the participant book as they watch.

Group Discussion

Video Discussion Questions

- Why is listening to God so important?
- Why do you think it is so hard for us to listen? What distracts us?
- How can we devour God's Word as Jeremiah did? How does devouring God's Word help us listen to God?
- What are three questions we should ask when approaching God's Word?
- Why does God want us to cling to Him like underwear? What can help us be close, intimate, and daily in our relationship with God?

Participant Book Discussion Questions

> *Note: Page references are provided for those questions that relate to specific questions or activities in the participant book.*

Before you begin, invite volunteers to look up the following Scriptures and be prepared to read them aloud when called upon. You might want to write each of the Scripture references on a separate note card or sticky note that you can hand out.

Scriptures: Jeremiah 7:13, 24-28; Jeremiah 9:20; Jeremiah 44:24-26; Mark 4:24-25; Hebrews 12:25-27; Jeremiah 31:35-37; Jeremiah 32:17-20; Jeremiah 50:33-34; Luke 19:41-44; Matthew 7:15-20; Jeremiah 23:16-32; Jeremiah 23:35; Jeremiah 33:3

Day 1: Called to Listen

- Have volunteers read aloud Jeremiah 7:13, 24-28; 9:20; and 44:24-26. How did God try to get through to His people? How has God spoken to you through His Word, circumstances, and His messengers? (page 75)
- Have volunteers read aloud Mark 4:24-25 and Hebrews 12:25-27. Would anyone be willing to share your one-sentence summary of these passages? (page 76) According to Mark 4:24-25, what did Jesus say about the importance of listening and the detriment of refusing to listen?

Day 2: Reading with Curiosity

- Take turns reading one verse each from Jeremiah 18:1-12. What are some things you learn about God from this passage? (page 78)
- How can you relate to being the clay that can't understand what it is being made into during the spinning, molding, and firing process? What kind of clay are you right now? (page 79)
- Does anyone in your group have experience with pottery? Does she have any insights to share related to the process?
- Have volunteers read aloud Jeremiah 31:35-37; 32:17-20; and 50:33-34. Do these passages that reveal the character of God encourage you to want to listen to Him more carefully? Why or why not? (page 80)

Day 3: Cling Like Underwear

- Have group members turn to Jeremiah 13:1-11 and read one verse each, going around until all the verses have been read. (You may have to go around again.) How is this illustration surprising or unusual? What main message do you think God is trying to get across?
- Which statement that you checked best describes where you are with Christ right now? (page 82) What factors in your life have contributed to why you chose that statement? Which statement would you like to describe your walk with Jesus? What would it take to get there?
- Reread Jeremiah 13:11 and also verse 17 aloud to the group. Then have someone read aloud Luke 19:41-44. How do these words of Jesus parallel Jeremiah 13:11, 17? (page 84)

Day 4: The Right Voices

- What are some of the broad messages that you find our culture speaking that don't necessarily line up with God's Word?

- What was the first insight given for discerning which voices we should heed? (page 86) Have someone read aloud Matthew 7:15-20. What two examples did Jesus use to describe false prophets? (page 87)
- What was the second insight? (page 87) Have someone read aloud Jeremiah 23:16-32. How did you describe straw and grain? What is the difference between them? (page 88)
- Read aloud the paragraph that begins "I find 'straw' creeping into my spiritual diet at times" (page 88). Which voices speaking into your life are more often "straw" rather than "grain"? Which sometimes become soul "junk food" for you? (Refer to the exercise on page 89 for ideas.)
- What is the third insight? (page 91) Have someone read aloud Jeremiah 23:35. What are some other questions you believe are beneficial in seeking to discern God's truth amid the many voices in your life?

Day 5: Keep Asking

- Have someone read aloud Jeremiah 33:3. What questions do you have for God right now? (page 94)
- Read aloud three paragraphs found on pages 94-95, beginning with "When I was in junior high" and ending with "Since teaching them ACTS, it has helped them learn to connect with God on a deeper level." What are some ways you were taught to pray as a child? How can you incorporate the discipline of listening into your prayer time?
- What did you hear God speaking to you during your asking/listening experience with God (Talk with God, page 97)?

Optional Group Activity (for a session longer than 60 minutes)

Choose one of the following activities:

1. Play-Doh® Creations

Purchase individual Play-Doh® containers (one for each woman in your group). Pass out the containers and say something like this:

Take this Play-Doh® and shape it into anything you like. Even if you don't consider yourself artistic, just make something as simple or as elaborate as you choose. God is the ultimate Potter, shaping and molding us into who He wants us to be. Think about Him as you shape your dough into your design. Play "The Potter's Hand" by Darlene Zschech (or another song) in the background, allowing about five minutes for the women to work on their creation. Then ask them to share with the group what they made and why. After everyone has shared, pick a few of these questions to discuss:

- What about the Play-Doh® made it easy or difficult to mold?
  - During part of the forming process, did your creation look nothing like the finished product?
  - How do you feel about what you have made?
  - What uses could your creation have?

End the activity by asking each woman to take home her creation and put it in a place where she will see it each day this week as a reminder to be patient and like soft clay, listening intently to God.

2. The Telephone Game

Whisper this sentence into the ear of the woman next to you:

Jeremiah listened to God instead of the voices of his culture and clung to God like underwear.

Instruct her to whisper it to the woman next to her. Keep going in this fashion, having the last woman say out loud what she heard. Then pick a few of these questions to ask:

- Did the end statement resemble the original one?
- Why is it sometimes best to go directly to the source of a statement?
- How have you seen information altered as it gets further from its original source?
- How can we apply this to listening to God in His Word and in prayer?

End by saying something like this:

It's funny when a statement is altered when playing a game. But it's less than comical when truths about God are altered. This happened in Jeremiah's day when even the priests and many prophets were saying things about God that weren't true. While it is beneficial to learn from our churches, leaders, and teachers, we also need to go directly to God and His Word to listen to what He has to say to us.

Prayer Requests

End by inviting the group members to share prayer requests and pray for one another. Use index cards, popcorn prayer, or another prayer technique included in "Tips for Tackling Five Common Challenges" (page 14) to lead this time with intentionality and sensitivity.

DIGGING DEEPER
WEEK 3 HIGHLIGHTS

Cultural Cues

See AbingdonWomen.com/Jeremiah for the full article.

This article looks at the economic and political parallels as well as the social and religious ideas in Jeremiah's time and ours.

Economic Crisis

Judah suffered economically during all the years that Jeremiah prophesied. Josiah ruled during Jeremiah's early years of prophecy and enjoyed the most political and economic freedom because he followed God and made religious reforms. However, the Judean economy spiraled downward as the Egyptian pharaoh Neco deported Josiah's son and then designated Jehoiakim to rule in 609 B.C.

When Babylon came to Judah in 605 B.C., Nebuchadnezzar defeated Egypt and drained Judah of its treasure and young leaders. To add insult to injury, "Jehoiakim paid tribute to Nebuchadnezzar and served three years as a Babylonian vassal."[1] Eventually Jehoiakim rebelled against Babylon. Babylon struck back, but Judah held on for a few years. Jehoiakim's son, Jehoiachin, assumed the throne at his father's death but reigned just three months. In 597 B.C. the Babylonians seized Jerusalem, exiled many, and set up Zedekiah as king.[2] He, too, eventually refused to pay the exorbitant taxes, resulting in the destruction of Jerusalem in 586 B.C.

Judah's money troubles correlated to their rebellion against God. Though Babylon was God's instrument, God orchestrated the defeat (see Jeremiah 25:8-9). Although no military invasion has rendered our nation a vassal nation, we still face an impending economic crisis. Many believe this financial instability also stems from a lack of caution and obedience to God's messages. We have lived beyond our means and now are paying "tribute" in the form of interest to other nations.

Political Globalization

The Babylonian Empire under Nebuchadnezzar was the center of the world at that time. As the Assyrian and Egyptian powers weakened, Babylon sought to conquer and unite an empire through force. Nebuchadnezzar's lust for expansion and world dominance led to a vast kingdom that was a new world order in his day.

Judah tried to form alliances with Egypt and surrounding nations in the hopes of looking to collective power to overcome their fiscal enemies. God called His people to trust in Him instead of other nations for help, but they refused to listen.

America's globalization is not that of a tyrant taking the world by force. Still, a subtle undercurrent ushering in a global economy looms on the horizon. Yet the utopian world politicians fantasize about through the unity of nations is not possible on this side of heaven because of humanity's sinful nature. Judah looked to other nations for peace and ended up in exile. I pray we will learn from their mistakes and trust fully in the Lord of Heaven's Armies as we pray for our leaders, exercise our right to vote, and stay informed about what is going on in our country. May we be cautious not to view God through our politics but, instead, to understand our government through the lens of God's Word.

Social Materialism

Judah fell into obscurity and poverty in the days of Jeremiah. God's chosen people looked for security and fulfillment in things they could touch, taste, and feel. Their affection for the idols of their neighboring countries, lack of contentment, and desire for money evidences itself throughout Jeremiah's writings.

American culture parallels the social materialism of Judah's day. The prophets and priests were also political advisors to the kings. In today's political arena of lobbyists, Ponzi schemes, and big government, we see many whose lives are characterized by greed. Socially, many people define themselves based on their salary, neighborhood, car, and vacations. Those with less money often grasp for an appearance of wealth, using debt to maintain their outward status.

The times of Jeremiah found people looking to define themselves by what they owned as well. God cried out that the leaders of the day offered a superficial treatment for His people's mortal wound (Jeremiah 6:13-14; 8:11). Today the same thing happens as we look to material goods to fill the God-shaped hole in our hearts.

The people of Judah also crossed moral lines to fulfill their cravings for nice things. Today, people still oppress the poor in pursuit of wealth. Although the Bible finds no fault with wealth, it has much to say about the love of money and ultimate attachments to the things of this world (1 Timothy 6:10, 1 Corinthians 7:31).

Religious Pluralism

The descendants of Abraham deviated from their religious neighbors with their monotheist belief in only one God. All the surrounding nations practiced the polytheistic worship of many gods. God made it clear from the time of Creation that He was the one and only. His first two commandments given through Moses spoke of His exclusivity.

In Jeremiah's day a revival took place during King Josiah's reign. Workers found lost portions of the Book of Deuteronomy during Temple repairs that revealed how far the people had strayed from God's commands. While King Josiah attempted to remove the shrines and idolatry, it didn't fully take root in people's hearts. They continued the Temple sacrifices but enjoyed the practice of adding foreign idol worship as well as sacrifices to other deities. Their response to Jeremiah's call back to the true worship of Yahweh was essentially that they would do as they pleased.

The people forgot the days of old when they saw God intervene mightily and dared not participate in the idolatry and polytheism of their neighbors. Not only did they tolerate other gods and forms of worship by foreigners; they syncretized new gods into their worship of Yahweh. They began to see worship of only one God as outdated, narrow-minded, and laughable in the face of modern enlightenment by surrounding nations.

America's tolerance of every religious form and practice has tended in recent years to embrace all faiths except those that claim ultimate truth. Movies, music, and especially reality television mock the narrow-mindedness of Christ-following. Religious freedom is a basic tenet of our nation for which we are thankful. However, in many ways religious freedom and tolerance have seemed to cross the threshold into a kind of "mandatory pluralism" in our society.

Traditional Christians believe that Jesus is not one of many ways to know God; He is *the* way. The American church has experienced some small revival movements just as in the time of Josiah, yet a widespread repentance from our culture's moral decay hasn't taken root. The American church trends away from the teachings of sin and repentance in favor of messages about peace and abundant life, rather than rightly balancing the two.

Our religious climate resonates greatly with the days of Jeremiah:

> *Then the LORD said, "Broadcast this message in the streets of Jerusalem. Go from town to town throughout the land and say, 'Remember the ancient covenant, and do everything it requires.'"*
>
> Jeremiah 11:6

Amidst the religious pluralism of our culture, we need to remember the truths of the Bible and live out our faith in obedience.

---

1. J. Andrew Dearman, *The NIV Application Commentary: Jeremiah and Lamentations* (Grand Rapids: Zondervan, 2002), 31.

2. *Harper's Bible Dictionary*, Paul J. Achtemeier, general editor, "Jehoiachin" and "Jehoiakim" entries by Jeremiah Unterman (San Francisco: Harper & Row, 1985), 451-452.

Week 4

STAYING SPIRITUALLY SENSITIVE

Heart Issues

Memory Verse

> *"The human heart is the most deceitful of all things,*
> *and desperately wicked.*
> *Who really knows how bad it is?*
> *But I, the LORD, search all hearts*
> *and examine secret motives.*
> *I give all people their due rewards,*
> *according to what their actions deserve."*

Jeremiah 17:9-10

Digging Deeper

Read Digging Deeper Week 4, "Somewhere Along the Road," and note any interesting facts or insights you would like to share with the group. (See page 49 for highlights; read the full article online at AbingdonWomen.com/Jeremiah.)

Materials Needed

- *Jeremiah* DVD and DVD player
- Stick-on nametags and markers (optional)

- Valentine conversation heart candies OR construction paper, scissors, and markers for creating hearts (Group Activity)
- Writing paper and pens (Group Activity)
- Index cards (optional – Prayer Requests)

Session Outline

Note: Refer to the format templates on page 7 for suggested time allotments.

Welcome

Offer a word of welcome to the group. If time allows and you choose to provide food, invite the women to enjoy refreshments and fellowship. (Groups meeting for 60 minutes may want to have a time for food and fellowship before the official start time.) Be sure to watch the clock and move to the All Play icebreaker at the appropriate time.

All Play

Ask each group member to respond briefly to these questions: *What's the last romantic movie you saw? What did you like or dislike about it? Did it give an accurate picture of what real life is like regarding matters of the heart?*

Read aloud or paraphrase:

We are drawn to issues of the heart. With this spiritual organ we love God and people but also experience the pain and disappointments of life. Sometimes we don't even realize the emotions that are buried underneath the surface. Have you ever found yourself feeling down or upset and you didn't even know why? (Pause briefly for responses.) God offers us great hope when we surrender our hearts to Him and enjoy the fellowship He created us to have. He doesn't ask us to walk our spiritual heart journeys alone, though. He places other people in our lives as examples and partners as we pursue God together. Let me share with you the highlights of what I learned from the Digging Deeper article for this week, "Somewhere Along the Road."

Digging Deeper Insights

Share insights from Digging Deeper Week 4, "Somewhere Along the Road." You might consider sharing the following:

- Jeremiah was influenced by others who had gone before him. (Hosea)
- He had one friend who followed God with him. (his scribe Baruch)
- He influenced those who would come after him. (Daniel)

Then ask: *When it comes to pursuing God's heart, who are the people you see as being a little farther down the road? Who are those running alongside you at a similar pace? Who are those you are looking to impact?* If you choose, encourage group members to read the full article online (AbingdonWomen.com/Jeremiah).

Prayer

Before playing the video segment, ask God to prepare the group to receive His Word and to hear His voice.

Video

Play the video for Week 4. Invite participants to complete the Video Viewer Guide for Week 4 in the participant book as they watch.

Group Discussion

Video Discussion Questions

- According to Proverbs 4:23, why do we need to guard our hearts?
- What is a spiritual heart check? Why is it important for us to take time to evaluate our hearts?
- What are some of the heavy heart clothes we often wear? Which of these heavy heart clothes is more of a challenge to you personally?
- What does God say about our hearts in Jeremiah 17:9? Why is it dangerous to follow our hearts?
- Once we've evaluated our hearts, what are we to do next?
- Why is behavior modification not real heart change? How does real heart change happen?
- What happens when God changes our hearts, giving us new hearts?

Participant Book Discussion Questions

Note: Page references are provided for those questions that relate to specific questions or activities in the participant book.

Before you begin, invite volunteers to look up the following Scriptures and be prepared to read them aloud when called upon. You might want to write each of the Scripture references on a separate note card or sticky note that you can hand out.

Scriptures: Jeremiah 2:35; Jeremiah 5:3; Jeremiah 8:6; Jeremiah 44:9-10; Psalm 139:23-24; James 5:16; Jeremiah 6:22-26; Mark 9:49; 1 Corinthians 3:12-15; 1 Peter 1:7; Jeremiah 6:15; Jeremiah 8:12; Proverbs 4:23; 2 Corinthians 10:5; 2 Chronicles 16:9; Psalm 103:1

Day 1: Heart Evaluation

- Have volunteers read aloud Jeremiah 2:35; 5:3; 8:6; and 44:9-10. After each selection is read, invite group members to share how they completed the corresponding "be careful" statement. (page 102)
- Is anyone willing to share the picture you drew of your heart with the kind of walls that are around it and tell us about it? (page 103)
- What adjectives did you check that describe your personal heart climate? (pages 105-07) Would you choose different adjectives today? What does that reveal about the heart's tendency to change?
- Have someone read aloud Psalm 139:23-24. How can this type of heart-honesty draw you closer to God?

Day 2: Behavior Modification vs. Heart Change

- Have group members turn in their Bibles to Jeremiah 3:12-25. Have each woman read one verse, going around until all the verses have been read. (You may have to go around again.) What part of the Know It, Share It, Own It message from the passage most resonates with you? (Refer to content on pages 110-114.)
- Have someone read aloud James 5:16. In the activity on page 113, did God bring anyone to mind that you need to meet with as a step toward healing in the relationship? Without sharing names or details, share about God's humbling work and your next steps toward reconciliation.
- As you read through Jeremiah 3:12-25, what character qualities of God did you find? (page 115)
- We won't read through this passage, but what heart insights did you glean from Jeremiah 4:3-22? (pages 115-116)

Day 3: Where Do Broken Hearts Go?

- Have someone read aloud Jeremiah 6:22-26. The illustration of heart pain in these verses is that of a woman in labor. Ask a mother in the group to share briefly about her childbirth experience. (You might want to choose this person in advance and talk with her before the session, giving some guidelines.) Can anyone relate to this kind of anguish in her heart today? Can anyone remember a time of deep anguish in the past? What is God's posture toward mourning in this passage? What is the difference between mourning and self-pity?

- Read aloud three paragraphs found on page 119, beginning with "Today in the West we live like ducks on the water" and ending with "They lacked faith in His power to really do something." What is the first thing you do when you are upset about something? Where do you turn?
- Have volunteers read aloud Mark 9:49; 1 Corinthians 3:12-15; 1 Peter 1:7. What are some things you learn about fire and trials from these verses? How do you think God wants to use your current trials to refine you? (page 120)
- Share a favorite verse you cling to when you are struggling (Talk with God, page 121).

Day 4: Guard Your Heart

- Have volunteers read aloud Jeremiah 6:15 and Jeremiah 8:12. What had Israel forgotten how to do? (page 122) How do you think we lose our shock factor today?
- Have someone read aloud Proverbs 4:23. What insights did you glean from considering how outside influences can positively and negatively affect your heart? (page 123)
- What are some practical ways we can guard our hearts from negative influences? (page 124)
- Have someone read aloud 2 Corinthians 10:5. What thought patterns need to be locked up in your life? (page 125)

Day 5: With All Your Heart

- Have group members turn in their Bibles to Jeremiah 24:1-10. Have each woman read one verse, going around the room until all the verses have been read. (You may have to go around again if your group is small.) What do you believe God is trying to communicate through the illustration of the figs? (Group members may find it helpful to refer to page 127.) How can this be applied in your life?
- From the chart contrasting Zedekiah and Jeremiah, what stands out to you about the attitudes and actions from the overflow of their hearts? (page 128)
- Have volunteers read aloud 2 Chronicles 16:9 and Psalm 103:1. How do these verses motivate you to pursue God wholeheartedly? What practical steps can you take? (page 130)
- Which heart caution did you circle that spoke most loudly to you personally? (page 130)

Optional Group Activity (for a session longer than 60 minutes)

Purchase some conversation heart candies. (Order online if out of season.) Divide into groups of 3-4 women, giving each woman two conversation heart candies. (If your group is small, you can work in pairs.)

Ask the women to put their sayings together and come up with a poem or story using the messages written on their hearts. Give them about ten minutes to laugh and work together. When they are finished, have each group share their poem or story. Then wrap up by saying something like this:

While we laughed and had fun with the words written on these candy hearts, we don't always have such good messages written on our own hearts. We carry pain from the hurtful words of others, the shame of our past sins, and the negative self-talk that often plays on a continuous loop. God wants to give us a new heart—His own. He wants to write His story on our hearts. As we conclude this week, I pray we will surrender our hurting hearts to Him and exchange them for hearts that have His words written on them.

If you don't have time to order candy hearts, you can make construction paper hearts and write on them some of the traditional sayings we find on conversation hearts, such as Luv u, Be mine, True Love, and many others.

Prayer Requests

End by inviting the group members to share prayer requests and pray for one another. Use index cards, popcorn prayer, or another prayer technique included in "Tips for Tackling Five Common Challenges" (page 14) to lead this time with intentionality and sensitivity.

DIGGING DEEPER
WEEK 4 HIGHLIGHTS

Somewhere Along the Road

See AbingdonWomen.com/Jeremiah for the full article.

Jeremiah's journey with God looked more like a marathon than a sprint. It required endurance, training, and other people cheering him on for him to make it to the finish line. Jeremiah felt alone at times, just as we all do, but he looked to those who had run before him as examples. In addition, he had spiritual running partners along the road. The legacy of his race also left a model for those who came behind him. Let's consider each of these aspects of Jeremiah's journey.

First, Jeremiah studied the writings of the prophets who went before him. His writings reveal the particular influence of the prophet Hosea. Though Hosea prophesied one hundred years before Jeremiah's ministry, Jeremiah could identify with him greatly because they both spoke God's harsh messages for an unrepentant people just before they were taken into exile. We, too, need to consider those who have trod the path we walk on now. Others who had similar experiences can challenge and encourage us. God wants us to seek out encouragement and wisdom just as Jeremiah did.

Second, Jeremiah looked around to see who was running beside him. He found a friend in his scribe, Baruch. Baruch worked closely with Jeremiah, which sometimes put him in danger. They had to hide together while facing arrest for going against the king to get God's messages to the people (Jeremiah 36:26). When Baruch whined about all their troubles, Jeremiah reminded him to seek God's glory and not his own (Jeremiah 45:1-5).

We, too, need to find others who are following God at a similar pace. When life gets tough, a godly friend can stand with us through difficult times. A good friend also helps pull us along when we start slowing our pace or going the wrong way. Everyone needs a "Baruch running buddy" to finish the race.

Finally, Jeremiah left a model for those who would follow. After the majority of his race was over, others took him against his will to Egypt where he ultimately died; yet his legacy lived on for those who would read his words. Daniel read Jeremiah's words to help him understand God's timeline of captivity (Daniel 9:2). Jesus saw the fulfillment of some of Jeremiah's specific prophecies lived out in regard to Herod and Judas (Matthew 2:17; 27:9). We also are part of that legacy. As we study and read about Jeremiah's life, we can learn from his failures and faith.

Week 5

QUITTING
THE BLAME GAME

Personal Responsibility

Memory Verse

> *This is what the LORD says:*
> *"Don't let the wise boast in their wisdom,*
>   *or the powerful boast in their power,*
>   *or the rich boast in their riches.*
> *But those who wish to boast*
>   *should boast in this alone:*
> *that they truly know me and understand that I am the LORD. . . ."*
>
> Jeremiah 9:23-24

Digging Deeper

Read Digging Deeper Week 5, "Royal Responsibility," and note any interesting facts or insights you would like to share with the group. (See pages 56-57 for highlights; read the full article online at AbingdonWomen.com/Jeremiah.)

Materials Needed

- *Jeremiah* DVD and DVD player
- Stick-on nametags and markers (optional)

- One recipe card for each group member and pens (find free printable recipe cards here: http://www.pinterest.com/spoelstras/jeremiah-bible-study-helps/) (Group Activity)
- Index cards (optional – Prayer Requests)

Session Outline

Note: Refer to the format templates on page 7 for suggested time allotments.

Welcome

Offer a word of welcome to the group. If time allows and you choose to provide food, invite the women to enjoy refreshments and fellowship. (Groups meeting for 60 minutes may want to have a time for food and fellowship before the official start time.) Be sure to watch the clock and move to the All Play icebreaker at the appropriate time.

All Play

Ask each group member to respond briefly to this question: *What's a favorite recipe you can make from memory? It can be an appetizer, main dish, or dessert.*

Read aloud or paraphrase:

Imagine eating the different ingredients of chocolate chip cookies separately. A stick of butter, a mouthful of brown sugar, or a teaspoon of vanilla wouldn't taste very good independently; but put them together and you get something amazing! Likewise we have events in our lives that are beyond our control, as well as our responses and choices related to those circumstances. Together these mix together through God's mysterious work in our lives, blending, softening, and perhaps even going through the fire. The outcome can be God's great work in our lives, using even our difficulties for good. We only have control over our response to life's events. Do you sometimes wish you had more control over your circumstances? (Pause briefly for responses.) The kings of Judah during Jeremiah's time struggled with their posture toward the difficult things in their lives. Let me share the highlights of what I learned from the Digging Deeper article for this week, "Royal Responsibility."

Digging Deeper Insights

Share insights from Digging Deeper Week 4, "Royal Responsibility." You might consider sharing the following:

- E + R = O (Events + Response = Outcome)
- The kings during Jeremiah's day were all too familiar with the blame game and tried to manipulate human solutions; they responded to the "events" of their lives with pride and fear. Their outcomes tell us that maybe we should try something else. As we look at the hand that has been dealt us, let's take Jeremiah's message to heart and take personal responsibility for our responses. It is the only variable we can control.

Ask this question: As you consider the equation E + R = O in your life, do you sense God calling you to make any changes in your responses? If you choose, encourage group members to read the full article online (AbingdonWomen.com/Jeremiah).

Prayer

Before playing the video segment, ask God to prepare the group to receive His Word and to hear His voice.

Video

Play the video for Week 5. Invite participants to complete the Video Viewer Guide for Week 5 in the participant book as they watch.

Group Discussion

Video Discussion Questions

- Which of the steps in God's prescription for rest for the soul do you struggle with most? Why?
- Why is it so important for us to "stop"? What helps you do this?
- How are blaming and complaining related? How can "looking around" help us avoid blaming and complaining and find rest for our souls?
- Has there been a trial in your life that you now can see was not about you but about someone else?
- What is the "old, godly way," and how is surrender related to it?
- Is there anything you need to do or change in order to travel the path—to better live what you say you believe?
- What two side effects of following God's prescription for rest were mentioned? What other side effects have you experienced from following these guidelines in your own life?

Participant Book Discussion Questions

Note: Page references are provided for those questions that relate to specific questions or activities in the participant book.

Before you begin, invite volunteers to look up the following Scriptures and be prepared to read them aloud when called upon. You might want to write each of the Scripture references on a separate note card or sticky note that you can hand out.

Scriptures: Jeremiah 12:1; Galatians 6:7; Hebrews 12:5-12; Jeremiah 21:8-9; Jeremiah 9:23-24; Jeremiah 13:15-17; Jeremiah 45:1-5; Jeremiah 9:25-26; Romans 2:29; Jeremiah 14:1-10

Day 1: Good Discipline

- Have someone read aloud Jeremiah 12:1. What current or past seemingly unfair situation in your life did you identify? (page 136)
- Have someone read aloud Galatians 6:7. What lessons have you learned the hard way according to the sowing and reaping principle? (page 138)
- According to the chart on justice and mercy, how would you sum up (in 1-2 sentences) these verses about why God allowed the people to be defeated by Babylon and face hardships? (pages 139-40)
- Have someone read aloud Hebrews 12:5-12. How does today's lesson change your perspective about God's heart in what He is trying to accomplish in your life? (page 142)

Day 2: Finding a Target

- As you reviewed the descriptions of the people's behavior in the matching exercise on page 143, what similarities to our culture did you see? How can these behaviors or attitudes serve as a warning to us?
- Have group members turn in their Bibles to Deuteronomy 30:11-20. Have each woman read one verse, going around the room until all the verses have been read. (You may have to go around again.) What are some things you learn from this passage about God's desires for us?
- Have someone read aloud Jeremiah 21:8-9. Do you believe Jeremiah was familiar with Deuteronomy 30:11-20? Some scholars believe the scrolls discovered during Temple renovations under King Josiah might have been the Book of Deuteronomy. How do these truths about choosing life in both Jeremiah and Deuteronomy relate to our spiritual lives today?
- Review your list of the difficult things in your life with the stars beside those things that are out of your control. (pages 146–147) Did this exercise help you identify things you may be worrying about that aren't in your power to change? Did you find benefit in seeing what you might need to address that is in your power to change?

Day 3: Perilous Pride

- Have someone read aloud Jeremiah 9:23-24. This is our memory verse this week. Can anyone say it from memory? God says that some people are wise, powerful, and rich. This isn't wrong. What does God say these people shouldn't do with their wisdom, power, or wealth? What are we not to boast in? What is the only thing we should boast about? (page 151) What are some practical and appropriate ways to boast in the Lord?
- Have someone read aloud Jeremiah 13:15-17. What does God say our pride causes Him to do? (page 151) What is your reaction to God's words about pride in this passage? If you are a parent, can you relate to these feelings when your children are prideful and difficult to correct?
- Have someone read aloud Jeremiah 45:1-5. What were Baruch's complaints? (page 152) How does Jeremiah's reaction seem to you initially? How is his advice loving if you consider it in the bigger picture?
- What are some of your tendencies when pride creeps in? (page 153) What freedom do you find in confession?

Day 4: Going Through the Motions

- Have someone read aloud Jeremiah 9:25-26. God was not pleased with the people going through the motions of circumcision without a heart of worship behind it. Can you think of some modern religious ceremonies that can lose their meaning if we aren't careful?
- Have someone read aloud Romans 2:29. How does this passage give further insight into circumcision of the heart? (page 156)
- Brainstorm together as a group some of the spiritual expressions Christians practice. What spiritual truth lies behind these practices? Which do you personally find spiritually enriching?
- Which areas of spiritual life did you check that may have lost their freshness in connecting you with God? (page 157)
- What action steps of change in your religious routines is God calling you to implement? (page 158)

Day 5: Rescue with Repentance

- What are you crying out to God to rescue you from right now?
- Have someone read aloud Jeremiah 14:1-10. Have you ever experienced someone apologizing to you over and over for the same thing, but they didn't stop the hurtful action? How does this help you understand Jeremiah 14:1-10 better?

- What lies do you tell about yourself that cause you to tell lies about God? (page 162)
- As we end this week on blame, what was your biggest take-away?

Optional Group Activity (for a session longer than 60 minutes)

Ahead of time, purchase or print recipe cards. Ask each woman to write her own recipe for humility. Each person struggles with pride differently. The ingredients could be attitudes, spiritual practices, people, difficult circumstances, or times of rest and reflection. Refer back to the E + R = O. Some of our ingredients may be difficult things in our lives that God is using to humble us. Here is my own example:

Humility for Melissa Spoelstra

- 4 cups of parenting situations
- 2 drops of my daughters' alopecia
- 60 ounces of prayer
- 15 Tablespoons of God's Word
- 2 teaspoons of my foot in my mouth or flaws exposed
- 1 pint of rest
- 2 fluid ounces of serving others

Blend these ingredients together tenderly and patiently. Heat in the oven for this season of life. Serve immediately.

Give an opportunity for each woman to share her recipe, and take time to affirm each one.

Prayer Requests

End by inviting the group members to share prayer requests and pray for one another. Use index cards, popcorn prayer, or another prayer technique included in "Tips for Tackling Five Common Challenges" (page 14) to lead this time with intentionality and sensitivity.

DIGGING DEEPER
WEEK 5 HIGHLIGHTS

Royal Responsibility

See AbingdonWomen.com/Jeremiah for the full article.

E + R = 0

This equation evaded the understanding of the kings of Judah during Jeremiah's lifetime; and if we aren't careful, we will miss its meaning as well.

Events + Response = Outcome[1]

The first variable—Events—is beyond our control. Many events and circumstances in life just happen to us. We can't change them. While we cannot govern the circumstances we often find ourselves in, the second variable—Response—rests fully in our hands. Will we remain humble? Will we seek God's help? Will we trust in what we can't see? Will we blame others for our problems or accept harsh realities with faith in a loving God?

Together the E and the R define the ultimate Outcome in our lives. As we look at the lives of the kings of Judah during Jeremiah's ministry, we mostly see "what not to do" with the R. These kings had little control over their E. They were kings by birth, with great responsibility over a nation during a time of oppression. Let's take a look at how several kings' formulas played out. (For a complete overview of the kings during Jeremiah's ministry, see the full online article.)

Josiah (640-609 B.C.) – 2 Kings 22:1–23:30

Events	—Became king at age 8 (2 Kings 22:1; 2 Chronicles 34:1).
	—In 622 B.C. a manuscript was found during Temple repair revealing God's laws that were being broken.
Response	—Instituted political and religious reforms to return to following God.
	—Refused to listen to God's directions about not going to battle against Egypt.
Outcome	—Reforms were more outward than inward in the hearts of people.
	—Died in battle against Egypt for his failure to consult God about the battle (2 Kings 23:29-30; 2 Chronicles 35:20-24).

—Jeremiah composed the funeral songs for Josiah that the Israelites sang for centuries as laments for the good things Josiah had done (2 Chronicles 35:25).

Jehoahaz (609 B.C.) – 2 Kings 23:31-33; 2 Chronicles 36:1-4

Events	—Son of Josiah who reigned only three months because Pharaoh Neco deported him to Egypt, where he died.
Response	—He was anti-Egyptian, which is probably why he was chosen as king over his older brother Eliakim (Jehoiakim) when Josiah died (Jeremiah 22:10-12).
Outcome	—Jeremiah requested mourning for Jehoahaz and prophesied he'd not return from captivity.

Jehoiakim (609-598 B.C.) – 2 Kings 23:34–24:7; 2 Chronicles 36:5-8

Events	—Son of Josiah, set up as king by Pharaoh Neco.
	—In 605 B.C., Jehoiakim became a Babylonian vassal.
Response	—Pro-Egyptian.
	—"He did what was evil in the sight of the LORD his God" (2 Chronicles 36:5).
	—Known for his re-institution of idol worship.
	—Rebelled against Babylon in 605 B.C. to side with Egypt.
Outcome	—"Jehoiakim had been a failure as ruler on both domestic and international fronts."[2] (Jeremiah 22:11-13, 17).
	—Reigned eleven years until taken to Babylon in chains.

The circumstances in these kings' lives were by no means a piece of cake. How about you? They blamed everyone but themselves, tried to manipulate solutions, and responded with pride and the fear of people. Their outcomes tell us that maybe we should try something else. As we look at the hand that has been dealt us, let's take Jeremiah's message to heart and take personal responsibility for our responses. It is the only variable we can control. We can choose humility, obedience to God, ears that listen to God's messengers, and a soft heart. As you consider applying this formula in your life, focus more on the R than the E. It has a great impact on the O in your heart and mind today.

---

1. Jack Canfield, *The Success Principles: How to Get from Where You Are to Where You Want to Be* (New York: HarperCollins, 2005), 6.
2. Philip J. King, Jeremiah: *An Archaeological Companion* (Louisville: Westminister/John Knox, 1993), 21.

Week 6

FINDING THE SOURCE OF OUR HOPE

The Promised Messiah

Memory Verse

"For I know the plans I have for you," says the Lord. *"They are plans for good and not for disaster, to give you a future and a hope."*

Jeremiah 29:11

Digging Deeper

Read Digging Deeper Week 6, "J²," and note any interesting facts or insights you would like to share with the group. (See pages 63–64 for highlights; read the full article online at AbingdonWomen.com/Jeremiah.)

Materials Needed

- *Jeremiah* DVD and DVD player
- Stick-on nametags and markers (optional)
- Stamped envelope and sheet of stationery, one for each group member; basket (Group Activity)
- Index cards (optional – Prayer Requests)

Session Outline

Note: Refer to the format templates on page 7 for suggested time allotments.

Welcome

Offer a word of welcome to the group. If time allows and you choose to provide food, invite the women to enjoy refreshments and fellowship. (Groups meeting for 60 minutes may want to have a time for food and fellowship before the official start time.) Be sure to watch the clock and move to the All Play icebreaker at the appropriate time.

All Play

Ask each group member to respond briefly to this question: *What is something you are hoping will happen soon?*

Read aloud or paraphrase:

We hope our plans will come together and our children will follow Jesus. These things may or may not happen. But there are some things we hope for that we know will happen. We know Jesus will return. We know He loves us and has good plans for us. We can hope in God when everything is great and when all seems lost. Jeremiah foreshadowed the Messiah through His prophecy and his own representation as a biblical Christ-type. Can you think of similarities you've noticed between Jesus and Jeremiah? (Pause briefly for responses.) Let me share the highlights of what I learned from the Digging Deeper article for this week, "J².".

Digging Deeper Insights

Share insights from Digging Deeper Week 6, "J²." You might consider sharing:

- Interesting or unexpected similarities between Jeremiah and Jesus.
- The one thing that sets Jesus apart from Jeremiah—His divinity. Highlight that, while Jeremiah pointed to Christ as a foreshadowing, Jeremiah was a human being prone to sin just like you and me.

Then ask this question: *How has our study of Jeremiah deepened your walk with Jesus?* If you choose, encourage group members to read the full article online (AbingdonWomen.com/Jeremiah).

Prayer

Before playing the video segment, ask God to prepare the group to receive His Word and to hear His voice.

Video

Play the video for Week 6. Invite participants to complete the Video Viewer Guide for Week 6 in the participant book as they watch.

Group Discussion

Video Discussion Questions

- How did Jeremiah refer to the Messiah?
- How would you explain the gospel message? How does salvation extend to those who lived before Christ as well as those who came after?
- What are justification, sanctification, and glorification?
- Would you agree that often our greatest struggle is God's greatest triumph in our lives? Why or why not?

Participant Book Discussion Questions

> *Note: Page references are provided for those questions that relate to specific questions or activities in the participant book.*

Before you begin, invite volunteers to look up the following Scriptures and be prepared to read them aloud when called upon. You might want to write each of the Scripture references on a separate note card or sticky note that you can hand out.

Scriptures: Jeremiah 29:10-14; 1 Kings 8:46-51; Jeremiah 15:18-21; Jeremiah 23:5-8; Jeremiah 33:14-18; Jeremiah 31:31-37; Jeremiah 32:38-41; Lamentations 3:18-24

Day 1: An Audience of One

- What is your biggest fear right now? (page 171)
- Have group members turn in their Bibles to Jeremiah 26. Have each woman read two verses each until the end of the passage. (You may have to go around again.) According to the chart on page 172, which characters feared God and which feared people or circumstances?
- What made it difficult for the latter to fear God instead of people? What makes it difficult for you?

Day 2: Good Plans Ahead

- Have someone read aloud Jeremiah 29:10-14. How does seeing our memory verse in context change the way you view this often-quoted verse?
- Have group members turn in their Bibles to Jeremiah 31:1-14 and have each woman read one verse, going around the room until all of the verses have been read. (You may have to go around again if your group is small.) What are some hopeful things God promises for the people of Judah? (page 176) What are some good things you know God has ahead for you—either generally as found in Scripture or specifically in your life?
- Which of the passages on page 176 did you put a star beside to indicate that they resonated with you? How do they give you hope for your future? (page 177)
- How do the New Testament verses on pages 177-178 increase your faith in the God of hope?

Day 3: Hope that Brings Us Back

- Have someone read aloud 1 Kings 8:46-51. How does this passage about the opportunity to turn back to God even when sin has separated us from fellowship with Him bring you hope?
- Have you ever felt hopeless in your circumstances? Would one or two people be willing to share about a time when it seemed that nothing good could come out of your trials? (page 180) Looking back, can you see some good that God brought out of the difficulty? (depth of character, closer relationships, unexpected blessing, and so on)
- Have someone read aloud Jeremiah 15:18-21. Jeremiah is basically saying to God, "Sometimes it seems like You are here, and sometimes it seems like You aren't." Have you ever felt that way? (page 182)
- Can you share about a time when following God meant standing alone? Have you ever been excluded, gossiped about, questioned, or humiliated because of your values, beliefs, choices, or actions? (Or perhaps you lost friends, a job, or something else you valued because of your pursuit of Jesus.) How did God sustain you through this time? (page 183)

Day 4: The Promised Messiah

- Have volunteers read aloud Jeremiah 23:5-8 and Jeremiah 33:14-18. What are some characteristics of the promised Messiah? (page 185)
- Have group members take turns reading aloud the following verses: Romans 5:17-18, Romans 10:3-4, and 2 Corinthians 5:20-21. What did you learn about righteousness—how we are made right with God—according to these verses? (pages 185-86) How do these truths help you battle the shame and condemnation the enemy aims at you?

- Have someone read aloud Jeremiah 31:31-37. How does this message encourage you— especially knowing that we are living under the new covenant? (page 187)

Day 5: Full Access

- Have someone read aloud Jeremiah 32:39-41. How does Jesus fulfill these promises? What is holding you back from fully believing these promises and applying them in your current circumstances? (pages 190-91)
- What can you do to take even greater advantage of the full access to God that you have in Jesus? (page 192)
- Have someone read aloud Lamentations 3:18-24. What were some of the circumstances that caused Jeremiah to have to dare to hope? Where was his focus that brought hope even when his circumstances grew worse?
- As you look back over the six weeks of study, how have you grown in hope through your study of Jeremiah? Can you identify one "take-away" that you know will stay with you in the future?

Optional Group Activity (for a session longer than 60 minutes)

Provide each woman with a stamped envelope and sheet of stationery. Ask her to write a letter to herself, seal it in the envelope, and write her address on the outside. Collect the envelopes, saying you will mail them one month after the study.

Say something like this:

God does amazing things in our hearts and minds through His Word and through the teaching and fellowship we experience with other women. However, our fast pace in life causes us to move quickly into the next activity. Sometimes it's better to focus on one or two things we've learned and keep them continually before us rather than try to remember so many different truths. Ask God to help you as you write a letter to yourself to help you remember what God has taught you through this study. Include verses you'd like to remember, a nudge from the Holy Spirit, or just encouragement to continue to dare to hope even in the midst of your trials. When you've finished your letter, put it into the envelope and seal it. Then address it to yourself and place it in the basket at the front of the room.

Prayer Requests
End by inviting the group members to share prayer requests and pray for one another. Use index cards, popcorn prayer, or another prayer technique included in "Tips for Tackling Five Common Challenges" (page 14) to lead this time with intentionality and sensitivity.

DIGGING DEEPER
WEEK 6 HIGHLIGHTS

J²

See AbingdonWomen.com/Jeremiah for the full article.

Without God = Without Hope.

This formula found in Ephesians 2:12 reminds us of the true source of our hope. Six hundred years before Christ came to earth, God gave us a glimpse of the Savior He would send through the prophet Jeremiah. Many commentators make mention of the correlations between the prophet Jeremiah and the Messiah he foretold. (See the online article for a list of parallels.)

Jeremiah and Jesus brought a similar message. Both warned of the need to be careful with God's message, idolatry, listening, hard-heartedness, blaming, and disobedience. However, they both also pointed to hope in God. Jesus' life and Jeremiah's life correspond in many ways, but they diverge on one great point: Jeremiah was a sinful man used by God to draw His people back.

Although Christ preached a similar message, His divinity sets Him apart as One much greater than a prophet. He came to reconcile people to God. He said boldly in John 14:6 that He is the way, the truth, and the life. He is the only way to come back to God. Jeremiah spoke of Jesus long before He knew His name. In fact he exercised faith in Jesus by believing in God's promise to send the Messiah.

Jeremiah's likeness to Jesus puts him in the category of a Christ-type. He foreshadows the Messiah who is to come. The similarities between Jeremiah and Jesus are meant to point us to a fuller understanding of who Christ is so that we can know Him.

As a teen I had a quiet-time diary that had two sections. In the first you answered this question: "What is the Scripture saying?" In the second you wrote in response to this question: "How does this apply to my life today?" While I am grateful that doing devotions this way when I was young helped me read curiously and ask questions, I found it incomplete. Not every verse of Scripture has a direct application in daily life. Some passages of Scripture "apply to my life" in that they expand my view of God. As I know and understand Him more, my intimacy with Him increases. It may not be something I can write in two sentences in my diary, but it revolutionizes my walk over time as I grow deeper in my relationship with Him.

As we see Jeremiah's life as a Christ-type, we grow a bigger view of God in our hearts. He is the ultimate source of hope that Jeremiah is pointing toward. As we end our study of Jeremiah, I pray we have developed a deeper knowledge and intimacy with the One he typified, our Lord and Savior, Jesus Christ. Through both J's we are reminded of the hope that comes through God alone.

CPSIA information can be obtained
at www.ICGtesting.com
Printed in the USA
LVOW05s0818270916

506283LV00001B/1/P